KU-453-226

S00000689543

On Your
Bike

Ruth Thomson

Commissioned photography by
Chris Fairclough

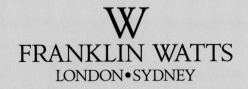

FRANKLIN WATTS
LONDON•SYDNEY

First published in 2004 by
Franklin Watts
96 Leonard Street
London
EC2A 4XD

Franklin Watts Australia
45-51 Huntley Street
Alexandria
NSW 2015

ISBN: 0 7496 5468 6

A CIP catalogue record for this book is available from the British Library

Printed in Malaysia
Planning and production by Discovery Books Limited
Editor: Helena Attlee
Designer: Ian Winton
Consultants: Alison Curtis, Manager of the Streetwise Safety Centre, Bournemouth,
Nevil Tillman, Bournemouth Road Safety Officer and Sharon Burn, teacher.

The author, packager and publisher would like to thank the following people for their
participation in this book: the Morwood family; Mike Spooner; James Wakelin, Matt Cooke
and other staff at Evans Cycles, Woking, to whom they are particularly grateful for the
generous loan of bikes and other equipment.

Contents

Off-road cycling

Joe loves cycling. He goes for cross-country rides near his home.

Joe has cycled along quiet roads and country lanes and paths, but he has never been on a busy town street.

Cycling Proficiency Test

Last month Joe passed his Cycling Proficiency Test at school. He proudly shows Mum his certificate and badge. 'Now you're ready to come cycling on the road with me,' Mum tells him.

Cycling Proficiency Test

If you want to cycle on the road, it is a good idea to do a Cycling Proficiency course.
You will learn how to:
- Start, dismount and park safely.
- Stop safely in an emergency.
- Make left and right hand turns.
- Cycle slowly without wobbling.
- Look after your bike.
- Choose suitable clothes for cycling.

You will also find out what different road signs mean.
You can find them all in a book called the *Highway Code*.

Checking the bike

Joe always looks after his bike very carefully. He knows how important this is.

The chain and the gears

Joe often cleans the dirty chain and gears with an old toothbrush. He squirts on chain oil to help the bike run smoothly.

The saddle height

When the saddle got too low, Mum adjusted it so that Joe's feet could just touch the ground.

The handlebars

Mum adjusts the handlebars as well, so that Joe's arms are slightly bent when he holds the handgrips and his knees do not hit the handlebars.

Tyres, lights and brakes

Mum helps Joe to check over the rest of his bike. 'Now you're going on the road, we must check your tyres, brakes and reflectors especially carefully,' she says.

They check that the wheels spin freely and that the tyres are firm.

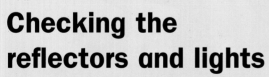

Checking the reflectors and lights

Joe cleans his reflectors. Bikes need a reflector at the front and back and one on each wheel. Joe also checks that the front and back lights work.

Testing the brakes

Mum tests Joe's brakes. The front inner brake cable is loose. They adjust it with the nut on the outer cable.

SAFETY FACTS

Brakes work when the calipers push the brake blocks against the wheel rim. Worn brake blocks will not stop a bike quickly enough in an emergency.

Adjusting nut

Brake cable

Caliper

Brake block

At the bike shop

Mum and Joe go to the bike shop to buy a new helmet.

Cycle helmets

The assistant fits Joe with a helmet. He shows him how to adjust the straps so it is secure. 'Wear this whenever you cycle - in playgrounds, parks or the garden, not just when you're on the road. And always replace it if it gets knocked in an accident,' he tells Joe.

Wearing a helmet correctly

A helmet should sit evenly between the ears and rest on the forehead – just above the eyebrows.

WRONG
Too far back.

WRONG
Too far forward.

RIGHT
Square on the head.

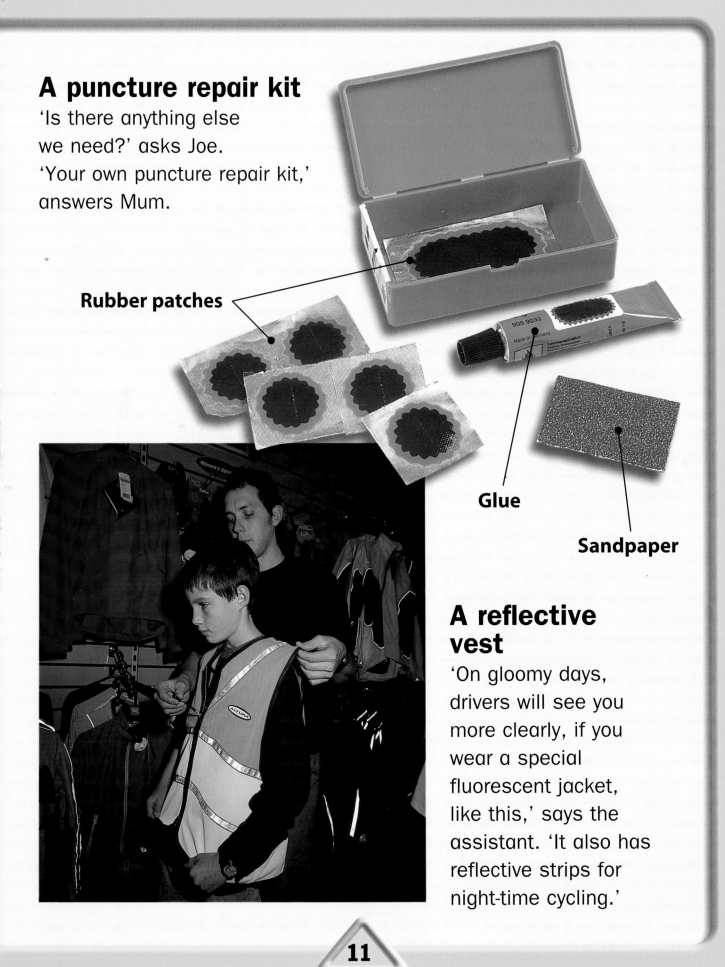

A puncture repair kit

'Is there anything else
we need?' asks Joe.
'Your own puncture repair kit,'
answers Mum.

Rubber patches

Glue

Sandpaper

A reflective vest

'On gloomy days,
drivers will see you
more clearly, if you
wear a special
fluorescent jacket,
like this,' says the
assistant. 'It also has
reflective strips for
night-time cycling.'

Getting ready for the trip

Joe and Mum plan a route that has roads with bike lanes and that avoids steep hills, dual carriageways and busy roundabouts.

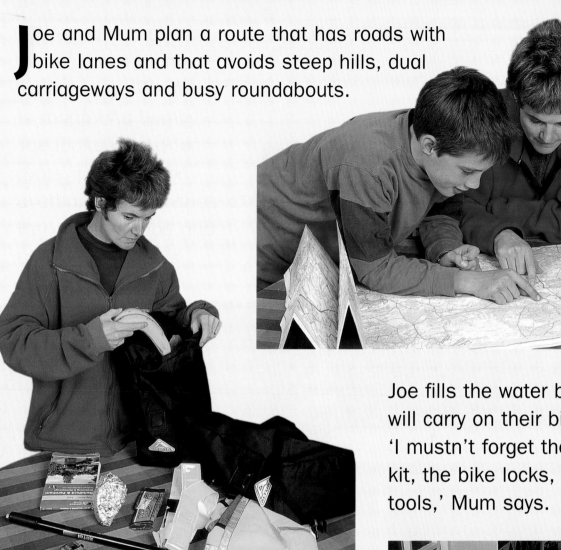

Joe fills the water bottles they will carry on their bikes. 'I mustn't forget the first-aid kit, the bike locks, lights and tools,' Mum says.

Supplies and equipment

Mum puts sandwiches, energy bars and bananas into her panniers, and packs waterproofs in case it rains.

- Carry light loads in a small rucksack.
- Carry heavy things in panniers on the bike.
- Never put bags over the handlebars. They could affect your steering or get tangled in the wheel.

Cycling clothes

'Can I wear these clothes?' asks Joe, in a dark top and flared trousers.

'It's better to wear bright or light-coloured clothes, so people can see you, and shorts, tracksuit bottoms or trousers that won't get trapped in the chain,' says Mum. 'And make sure your laces are tied properly.'

'How about these?' asks Joe.
'Much better,' says Mum.

Riding on the road

Joe wheels his bike to the kerb and lifts it on to the road, holding the front brake. He gets on from the pavement, making sure the pedal nearest the road is high, so he can get a good push off.

A safe start

Joe looks over his right shoulder, checking for traffic, and stretches out his right arm to show that he is ready to set off. When the road is clear, Joe starts cycling. Mum follows, so she can watch Joe.

Riding along

Mum reminds Joe to ride about half a metre away from the kerb. They watch out for potholes, gravel, puddles and rubbish. Joe uses his bell to warn pedestrians that he is coming.

SAFETY FACTS

Safe cycling reminders

- Keep both hands on the handlebars, except when signalling.
- Keep both feet on the pedals.
- Glance over your shoulder regularly.
- Keep your fingers near the brake levers, ready to stop.
- Ride in a straight line.
- Always wear a helmet.

Turning left and right

Soon they need to turn left.
Well before the T-junction, Joe
checks that there are no cars
behind him. It is all clear, so he
signals with his left arm.

Turning left

Just before the junction,
he puts both hands on
the handlebars and stops.
He waits for a gap in the
traffic before cycling
around the corner.

Turning right

Now they have to turn right. This is harder. Well ahead of the junction, Joe looks over his shoulder to make sure nothing is coming. He signals right and moves into the centre of the road.

Stopping at the junction

When they reach the main road, they stop because there is traffic coming. Once it has passed and there is a safe gap, they turn right safely.

SAFETY FACTS

- **Do not ride on the inside of cars slowing down to turn left.**
- **Lorries need plenty of room to turn corners. Wait until they have passed.**
- **Give way to pedestrians crossing the road.**

Busy roads

The main road is busy. Joe would rather cycle on the pavement where he thinks it is safer, but Mum says that this is against the law. 'Pavements are for pedestrians. You might hit someone,' she says.

Cycle lanes

Luckily there is soon a separate lane for cyclists. Joe feels safer cycling here. Cars and lorries are not allowed to drive or park in cycle lanes.

SAFETY FACTS

Look out for signs that tell cyclists where they can ride.

Overtaking

Further on, they have to ride on the road again. There is a line of parked cars ahead. 'Move well out to pass them,' shouts Mum, 'in case one of the drivers opens a car door in your path and you can't stop in time.'

SAFETY FACTS

Look out for car lights and indicators that tell you a parked car is about to pull out.

Roundabouts and parking

Joe and Mum
approach
a roundabout.
'We need to go
straight on here,'
says Mum.

Going straight on across at a roundabout

Approach a roundabout in the left–hand lane. Give way to traffic coming from your right and wait for a safe gap. Join the roundabout, watching out for cars behind you or those turning left in front of you. Stay in the left-hand lane and signal before your exit.

Parking

Mum and Joe come to some shops. Mum suggests they stop for an ice lolly. Joe rushes into the shop to choose one, leaving his bike lying on the pavement.

'That's not a good idea,' says Mum. 'Your bike is in the way of other shoppers. Someone could easily fall over it, especially someone who can't see very well.'

Joe stands his bike neatly against the shop wall instead.

Crossings

They come to a set of traffic lights. The lights have turned red, so they wait behind the stop line. When the lights turn amber, they position their pedals ready to push off.

When the lights turn green, they cycle away.

'Start off slowly,' advises Mum. 'You should always look around first to check that there are no pedestrians or cars still crossing your path.'

Zebra crossings

'Watch out,' says Mum, a little further on. 'There's a zebra crossing ahead.'

She can see the flashing Belisha beacons and zig-zag lines. These remind cyclists and drivers to slow down. 'You should always stop for pedestrians at crossings like this,' she says.

Crossings with traffic lights

Pelican, puffin and toucan pedestrian crossings have traffic lights. When the lights flash amber, you must give way to any pedestrians on the crossing, but you can cycle on if it is clear.

Time to eat

At last, they reach the canal. 'We can't cycle here,' says Mum, pointing to the sign. 'Why not?' says Joe. 'You might spoil other people's quiet stroll,' explains Mum, 'or possibly cause an accident.'

Cyclists Please Dismount

In the interests of all our visitors we kindly ask that cyclists dismount whilst in the Canal Centre grounds

Lock it!

They wheel their bikes to the picnic area and lock the frame and wheel on to a cycle rack.
Mum takes the panniers off her bike.
'We don't want to tempt a thief,' she says.

Keeping warm

After his ride, Joe is thirsty and hot.
'Put on another layer,' says Mum. 'You'll cool down very quickly now we've stopped, and you don't want to catch a cold.'

Refreshments

'All that cycling has made me very hungry,' says Joe, as they sit down to eat.

SAFETY FACTS

Cycling uses a lot of energy. Take snacks, such as bananas, chocolate or energy bars, to give you a quick boost, as well as plenty to drink.

Repairing a puncture

As they start to cycle home, Joe notices that his front tyre is flat. Mum takes out the repair kit.

Taking off the tyre

Mum shows Joe how to release the brake calipers and take off the wheel. She uses tyre levers to remove the tyre and runs her finger carefully around the inside. 'Here's the culprit,' she says, taking out a nail.

Finding the hole

'Pump up the tube,' says Mum, 'so you can find the hole by feeling and listening for escaping air.'

Mum finds the hole and roughens the area around it with the sandpaper.

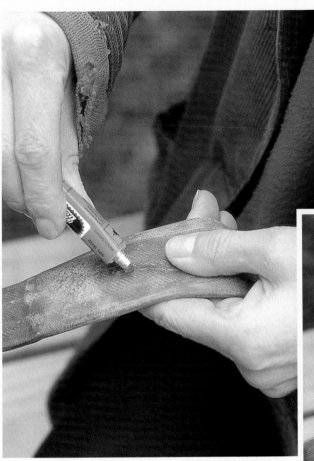

Patching the puncture

Mum spreads glue over the hole and presses on a patch to fix the puncture.

Refitting the tube

She carefully pushes the tube back inside the tyre. Then she slides the wheel back into place, tightens the bolts, pumps up the tyre fully and reconnects the brakes.

'All fixed!' she says.

Cycling in the countryside

They take a short cut home along a bridleway. The track is rough and bumpy. Joe looks ahead for roots, puddles and overhanging branches. He keeps a good grip on his handlebars.

PUBLIC BRIDLEWAY

SAFETY FACTS

Country roads

- Keep well to the left and ride in single file on narrow country roads.
- Listen out for cars – hedgerows may make it difficult for drivers to see you in advance.
- Watch out for bumps and potholes.

Home in the dark

It is starting to get dark as they approach home, so they stop to fit their lights and put on their reflective strips.

Lights

For cycling at night and on gloomy days, you must have a white light at the front and a red light and red reflectors at the back. Always check the batteries in your lights before you set off.

'That was great,' smiles Joe when they get home. 'Can we go for another ride next week?'

Glossary

Bridleway A wide path for pedestrians, cyclists and horse riders.

Cycling Proficiency Test A test carried out to prove that a cyclist has learnt the basic safety rules of cycling on the road.

Fluorescent A kind of material that is clearly visible from a long distance, because of the special way that it reflects light.

Highway Code A booklet issued by the government, setting out the laws and rules for pedestrians, cyclists, motorcyclists, horse riders and drivers on the road.

Junction The place where two roads meet.

Kerb The edge of a pavement where it meets a road.

Pannier A luggage bag that fits on to the carrying rack over the back wheel of a bicycle.

Pavement A raised walkway at the side of a road where people can walk safely.

Pedestrian Any person who walks.

Pedestrian crossing A specially designed crossing where people can cross a road safely.

Pelican crossing A crossing with traffic lights controlled by pedestrians.

Puffin crossing A pedestrian-friendly crossing with sensors that control the traffic lights.

Reflective A surface that reflects (sends back) light such as the light from a car's headlights.

Traffic lights Red, amber and green lights that change in a particular order, to tell traffic whether to stop or go.

Toucan crossing A crossing with traffic lights on a cycle route, where cyclists and pedestrians can cross at the same time.

Zebra crossing A pedestrian crossing with black and white stripes painted on the road and flashing Belisha beacons on stripy poles.

Useful addresses and websites

Bicycle Helmet Initiative Trust,
1st floor, 43-45 Milford Road, Reading,
Berkshire RG1 8LG
www.bhit.org

British Cycling/Go Ride,
National Cycling Centre, Stuart Street,
Manchester M11 4DQ
www.go-ride.org.uk
Runs an in-school cycle skills programme.
See website for details.

Child Accident Prevention Trust,
18-20 Farringdon Lane, London EC1R 3HA
www.capt.org.uk
Provides information on fitting cycle helmets
correctly and fact sheets on safe cycling.

Cyclists Touring Club (CTC),
69 Meadrow, Godalming, Surrey GU7 3HS
www.ctc.org.uk
National cycling organisation that promotes
bicycle travel and campaigns for cyclists.

Department for Transport,
Free Literature Services, PO Box 2367,
Wetherby LS23 7NB
For free literature, call 0870 1226 236
www.hedgehogs.gov/arrivealive
Provides advice on safe cycling in their free
booklet Arrive Alive.

Highway Code
www.roadcode.co.uk
This on-line version and booklet about the
Highway Code has been written for younger
road users.
www.highwaycode.gov.uk
The full contents of the Highway Code.

**Royal Society for the Prevention of
Accidents (RoSPA)**,
Edgbaston Park, 353 Bristol Road,
Birmingham B5 7ST
www.rospa.com
Provides guidance on cycle training.

Sustrans,
35 King Street, Bristol BS1 4DZ
www.sustrans.org.uk
Provides eight free information booklets on
cycling, covers topics such as basic bike
maintenance, cycling clothes and
accessories and choosing the right bike and
accessories.

The Child Accident Prevention Foundation
www.kidsafe.com.au
A nationwide Australian charity providing
lots of useful advice on the prevention of
accidents.

Child Safety Foundation
www.childsafety.co.nz
A New Zealand website designed mainly for
use by parents, which promotes all aspects
of pre-school and early primary school safety.

Note to parents and teachers
Every effort has been made by the Publishers to
ensure that these websites are suitable for
children, that they are of the highest educational
value, and that they contain no inappropriate or
offensive material. However, because of the
nature of the Internet, it is impossible to
guarantee that the content of these sites will not
be altered. We strongly advise that Internet
access is supervised by a responsible adult.

Index